INSIDE THE MINNESOTA VIKINGS

JOSH ANDERSON

Lerner Publications ◆ Minneapolis

Copyright © 2024 by Lerner Publishing Group, Inc.

All rights reserved. International copyright secured. No part of this book may be reproduced, stored in a retrieval system, or transmitted in any form or by any means—electronic, mechanical, photocopying, recording, or otherwise—without the prior written permission of Lerner Publishing Group, Inc., except for the inclusion of brief quotations in an acknowledged review.

Lerner Publications Company
An imprint of Lerner Publishing Group, Inc.
241 First Avenue North
Minneapolis, MN 55401 USA

For reading levels and more information, look up this title at www.lernerbooks.com.

Main body text set in Aptifer Slab LT Pro / Typeface provided by Linotype AG

Library of Congress Cataloging-in-Publication Data

Names: Anderson, Josh, author.
Title: Inside the Minnesota Vikings / Josh Anderson.
Description: Minneapolis, MN : Lerner Publications, [2024] | Series: Lerner sports. Super sports teams | Includes bibliographical references and index. | Audience: Ages 7–11 | Audience: Grades 4–6 | Summary: "The Minnesota Vikings have played in four Super Bowls, but they've never won the big game. With a talented roster and a hot new coach, the team's first championship might be right around the corner"— Provided by publisher.
Identifiers: LCCN 2022049970 (print) | LCCN 2022049971 (ebook) | ISBN 9781728491028 (library binding) | ISBN 9798765604052 (paperback) | ISBN 9798765601631 (ebook)
Subjects: LCSH: Minnesota Vikings (Football team)— History—Juvenile literature.
Classification: LCC GV956.M5 A64 2024 (print) | LCC GV956.M5 (ebook) | DDC 796.332/6409776579—dc23/eng/20221018

LC record available at https://lccn.loc.gov/2022049970
LC ebook record available at https://lccn.loc.gov/2022049971

Manufactured in the United States of America
1 – CG – 7/15/23

TABLE OF CONTENTS

NFL CHAMPIONS 4
LET'S GO, VIKINGS! 9
AMAZING MOMENTS 15
VIKINGS SUPERSTARS 19
SOUND THE GJALLARHORN 25

Vikings Season Record Holders 28
Glossary 30
Learn More 31
Index 32

Vikings linebacker Roy Winston (*center*) chases down Cleveland Browns quarterback Bill Nelsen (*right*) in the 1970 National Football League Championship game.

NFL CHAMPIONS

FACTS AT A GLANCE

- The **VIKINGS** made their first trip to the Super Bowl in 1970.

- During the 1970s, the team made four trips to the **SUPER BOWL**.

- In 1998, Minnesota had one of the highest-scoring teams ever. They scored **556 POINTS** during the regular season.

- From 1998 to 2001, the Vikings had two future **PRO FOOTBALL HALL OF FAME** wide receivers on the team at the same time.

The Minnesota Vikings faced the Cleveland Browns in 1970 in the National Football League (NFL) Championship. The Browns had one of the league's top offenses. The Vikings had a tough defense. Their defensive line was nicknamed The Purple People Eaters.

    The Vikings set a new team record with 12 wins that season. They defeated the Los Angeles Rams in the first round of the playoffs. The victory earned Minnesota their trip to the NFL Championship. If they could defeat Cleveland, the Vikings would play in the Super Bowl for the first time in team history.

Minnesota took an early 7–0 lead against Cleveland. With the Super Bowl on the line, the Vikings desperately wanted to score again. Quarterback Joe Kapp dropped back to pass from Minnesota's 25-yard line. At first, he didn't spot any open receivers. The Cleveland defense pushed closer and closer to Kapp, threatening a sack.

Kapp spotted wide receiver Gene Washington. The defender covering Washington slipped, leaving Washington wide open. Just before Cleveland's defenders reached Kapp, he lofted the ball high into the air. Washington caught the ball and ran 75 yards for a touchdown. The Vikings took a 14–0 lead on the play and never looked back.

Minnesota's defense held the Browns without a score until the fourth quarter. The Vikings kept scoring, and the team cruised to a 27–7 victory. Although the Vikings lost in the Super Bowl a week later, winning the NFL Championship was an exciting moment for the team and its fans.

Quarterback Joe Kapp turns to hand the ball to a running back in the 1970 NFL Championship game.

Defensive lineman Carl Eller (*center*) pushes past a Browns offensive lineman.

Vikings defensive end Jim Marshall practices in the snow. He played for the team from 1961 to 1979.

LET'S GO, VIKINGS!

When the team started, the Minnesota Vikings planned to play in the American Football League (AFL). The AFL was a new league created to compete for fans with the NFL. But when the NFL offered Minnesota's owners a place in the league, the owners changed their plans.

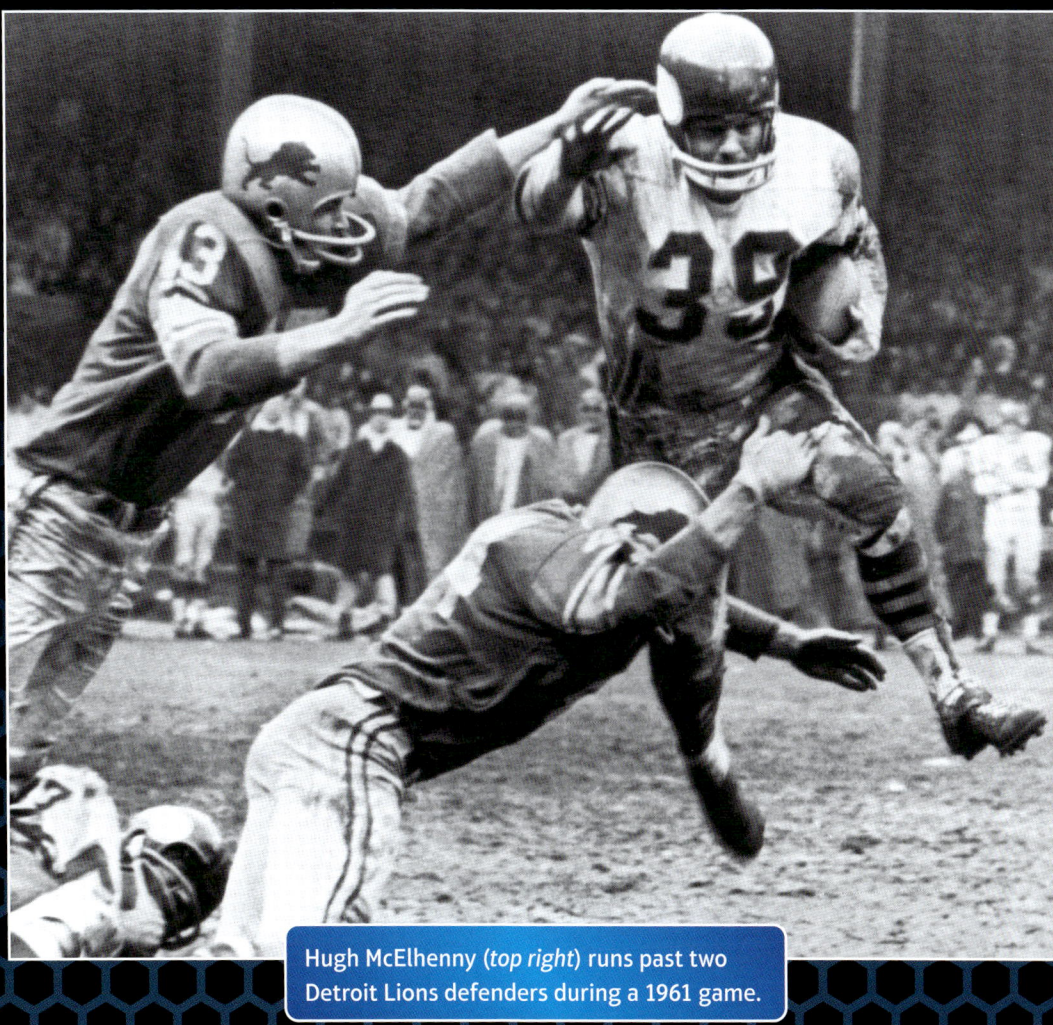

Hugh McElhenny (*top right*) runs past two Detroit Lions defenders during a 1961 game.

The Vikings started playing in the NFL in 1961. The team chose the name Vikings because many people in Minnesota have family histories that go back to northwestern Europe, where Vikings originated. Vikings were pirates who worked mostly off the coasts of Europe from the 8th to 11th centuries.

The team played its first 21 seasons in Metropolitan Stadium. The Vikings shared the building with Major League Baseball's Minnesota Twins.

Metropolitan Stadium in Bloomington, Minnesota, was the first home field for the VIkings.

VIKINGS FACT

The Vikings weren't the first NFL team from Minnesota. A team called the Marines, and later the Red Jackets, played in the league from 1905 until 1924.

Vikings quarterback Fran Tarkenton was the NFL's Most Valuable Player in 1975.

Before the team's first season, the Vikings chose quarterback Fran Tarkenton from the University of Georgia in the NFL Draft. Tarkenton started nearly every Vikings game during the team's first six seasons. He left for New York and played five seasons for the Giants. Tarkenton then returned to Minnesota for seven more seasons.

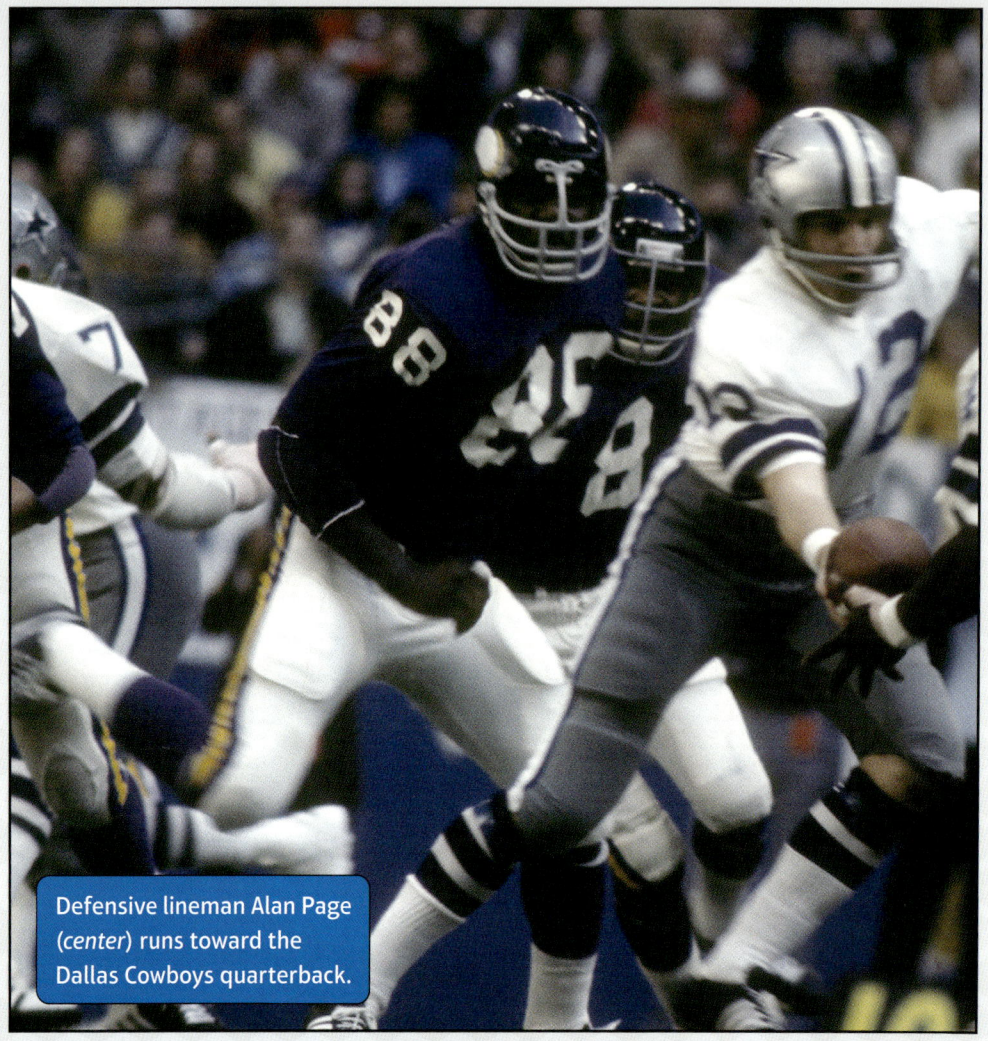

Defensive lineman Alan Page (*center*) runs toward the Dallas Cowboys quarterback.

Tarkenton was one of the NFL's top quarterbacks, but the Vikings didn't make the playoffs in any of their first seven seasons in the NFL. They only finished with a winning record once during that time.

Bud Grant became Minnesota's head coach in 1967. Grant's first season in Minnesota would be their last losing season for many years. The Vikings were about to begin the most successful period in team history.

Bud Grant coached the Vikings from 1967 to 1985.

The Vikings and Lions faced off in snowy, muddy conditions during a 1967 game.

AMAZING MOMENTS

The Purple People Eaters defensive line led the Vikings to a period of great success in the late 1960s and 1970s. In 1967, the Vikings set the NFL record by causing the Detroit Lions to fumble 11 times in one game.

The Vikings finished in first place in the NFL Central Division for the first time in 1968. They played in their first playoff game that year but lost to the Baltimore Colts. The following year, the Vikings finished first in the division again. They also earned their first trip to the Super Bowl. But the Vikings lost the 1970 Super Bowl to the Kansas City Chiefs 23–7.

Vikings running back Dave Osborn (*center left*) fights for yards against the Kansas City Chiefs in the 1970 Super Bowl.

The Vikings finished in first place in their division eight times in the 1970s. They played in a total of four Super Bowls during that decade. But Minnesota could not manage to win the big game.

Although the Vikings have not played in the Super Bowl since 1977, Minnesota fans have enjoyed many exciting years. The Vikings had one of the greatest seasons of all time in 1998. The team finished with a 15–1 record. The team's high-powered offense scored 556 points. Only five teams have ever scored more in a single season. The Vikings barely missed out on the Super Bowl that year. They lost the 1999 NFC Championship game 30–27 to the Atlanta Falcons.

Even though the Vikings did not make the playoffs in 2007, fans were treated to a record-breaking performance during a home game against the San Diego Chargers. Running back Adrian Peterson rushed for 296 yards in the game. That's the most ever in one game in NFL history.

Quarterback Randall Cunningham threw 34 touchdown passes during Minnesota's 1998 season.

After signing future Hall of Fame quarterback Brett Favre, Minnesota won the NFC Central Division in 2009. They made it back to the NFC Championship game in 2010 but missed making the Super Bowl by just three points. They lost 31–28 to the New Orleans Saints.

The team's best season in recent years was in 2017. The Vikings won their division with a 13–3 record and advanced to the NFC Championship game. This time, the Philadelphia Eagles beat the Vikings 38–7.

VIKINGS FACT

The Vikings and the Rams are the only two teams to play in at least one NFC Championship game in every decade from the 1970s to the 2010s.

In 2017, quarterback Case Keenum almost led the Vikings to the Super Bowl in his only season with the team.

Wide receiver Cris Carter led the NFL with 122 catches in 1994.

VIKINGS SUPERSTARS

Minnesota has been home to many superstar players over the years. Quarterback Fran Tarkenton played 13 seasons for the Vikings. He's the team's all-time leader in passing yards, passing touchdowns, and completed passes. The Hall of Famer also led the team to the Super Bowl three times in the 1970s.

Quarterback Fran Tarkenton stands behind Minnesota's offensive line during the 1977 Super Bowl.

Defensive linemen Carl Eller and Alan Page both entered the Hall of Fame after their playing days. Eller and Page were the biggest stars of the fearsome Purple People Eaters defensive line in the 1960s and 1970s. They teamed up with Pro Bowl players Jim Marshall and Gary Larsen to make things difficult for opposing teams. After retiring from football, Page went on to become an associate justice on the Minnesota Supreme Court. He was the first Black person ever to serve on that court.

Alan Page sets his sights on the Chicago Bears quarterback.

> **VIKINGS FACT**
> Before his coaching days, Bud Grant played in both the NFL and the National Basketball Association.

Offensive lineman Randall McDaniel (*left*) holds off a Cincinnati Bengals defender.

Head coach Bud Grant led the Vikings for 18 seasons. He guided Minnesota to 158 regular season wins and four Super Bowl appearances. Randall McDaniel was one of the fastest offensive linemen to ever play in the NFL. A member of the Vikings from 1988 to 1999, the Hall of Famer was a Pro Bowl player in 11 of his 12 seasons with the team.

From 1998 to 2001, the Vikings had two future Hall of Fame wide receivers on the team at the same time. Cris Carter finished his Vikings career as the team's leader in receiving yards and receiving touchdowns. His 130 receiving touchdowns rank fourth in NFL history.

Wide receiver Randy Moss reaches out to catch a long pass in a game against the Indianapolis Colts.

The last four seasons of Carter's time with the Vikings overlapped with the first four seasons for Randy Moss. Moss was incredibly skilled all over the field, but his size and strength made him almost unstoppable near the goal line. Moss led the NFL in receiving touchdowns three times while playing in Minnesota. He ranks second in NFL history with 156 career receiving touchdowns. Moss also ranks fourth in career receiving yards.

Defensive lineman John Randle played 11 seasons for the Vikings from 1990 to 2000. He was a Pro Bowl player six times with Minnesota. Randle led the league in sacks in 1997 with 15.5. He is a member of the Pro Football Hall of Fame.

Adrian Peterson is one of the greatest running backs to ever play the game. He led the league in rushing three times with the Vikings. His 2,097 rushing yards in 2012 are the second most in a single season. He ranks fourth all-time in rushing touchdowns and fifth all-time in rushing yards.

Adrian Peterson is Minnesota's all-time leader with 11,747 rushing yards.

Wide receiver Justin Jefferson was a Pro Bowl player after each of his first two seasons in the NFL.

SOUND THE GJALLARHORN

In 2016, the team began playing in U.S. Bank Stadium. Before every home game, a special guest sounds the Gjallarhorn (YAH-ler-horn). The Gjallarhorn is a huge musical instrument based on a horn from Viking mythology.

The Vikings missed out on the playoffs in 2020 and 2021. But the team and its fans are hopeful for the future. They have two of the NFL's most exciting offensive players. The Vikings chose wide receiver Justin Jefferson in the first round of the 2020 NFL Draft. In 2020 and 2021, Jefferson combined for 3,016 yards. That's the most receiving yards ever in a player's first two seasons. Running back Dalvin Cook has rushed for over 1,000 yards in a season three times and has played in three Pro Bowls.

It's a special honor to sound the Gjallarhorn before a Vikings home game.

Leading the offense is quarterback Kirk Cousins. He is one of the most accurate passers in football. Cousins ranked in the top 10 in passing yards in three of his first four seasons in Minnesota.

Although the Vikings struggled on defense in 2020 and 2021, their top defensive player is one of the best safeties in the league. Harrison Smith has logged 33 interceptions in his career and has been a Pro Bowl player six times. The Vikings chose defensive players Lewis Cine and Andrew Booth Jr. in the 2022 NFL Draft. The team also signed Pro Bowl defensive end Za'Darius Smith. He will pair with another Pro Bowl player, Danielle Hunter, on the Minnesota defensive line.

The team hired a new head coach for the 2022 season. Kevin O'Connell worked for the Los Angeles Rams when they won the Super Bowl in 2022. In Minnesota, he's an NFL head coach for the first time. With their high-powered offense and some new faces on defense, fans have good reason to believe O'Connell can lead the Vikings back to the Super Bowl for the first time since 1977.

Dalvin Cook (*center*) rushed for 16 touchdowns during the 2020 NFL season.

Quarterback Kirk Cousins helped lead the Vikings to the playoffs in 2019.

Wide receiver Adam Thielen grew up in Minnesota before becoming a member of the Vikings.

VIKINGS SEASON RECORD HOLDERS

RUSHING TOUCHDOWNS
1. Adrian Peterson, 18 (2009)
2. Dalvin Cook, 16 (2020)
3. Chuck Foreman, 13 (1975)
   Chuck Foreman, 13 (1976)
   Terry Allen, 13 (1992)
   Dalvin Cook, 13 (2019)

RECEIVING TOUCHDOWNS
1. Cris Carter, 17 (1995)
   Randy Moss, 17 (1998)
   Randy Moss, 17 (2003)
2. Randy Moss, 15 (2000)
3. Adam Thielen, 14 (2020)

PASSING YARDS
1. Daunte Culpepper, 4,717 (2004)
2. Kirk Cousins, 4,298 (2018)
3. Kirk Cousins, 4,265 (2020)
4. Warren Moon, 4,264 (1994)
5. Warren Moon, 4,228 (1995)

RUSHING YARDS
1. Adrian Peterson, 2,097 (2012)
2. Adrian Peterson, 1,760 (2008)
3. Dalvin Cook, 1,557 (2020)
4. Robert Smith, 1,521 (2000)
5. Adrian Peterson, 1,485 (2015)

PASS COMPLETIONS
1. Kirk Cousins, 425 (2018)
2. Sam Bradford, 395 (2016)
3. Daunte Culpepper, 379 (2004)
4. Warren Moon, 377 (1995)
5. Kirk Cousins, 372 (2021)

SACKS
1. Jared Allen, 22 (2011)
2. Chris Doleman, 21 (1989)
3. Keith Millard, 18 (1989)
4. John Randle, 15.5 (1997)
5. Chris Doleman, 14.5 (1992)
   Jared Allen, 14.5 (2008)
   Jaren Allen, 14.5 (2009)
   Danielle Hunter, 14.5 (2018)
   Danielle Hunter, 14.5 (2019)

GLOSSARY

defensive end: a player whose main jobs are to rush the quarterback and defend rushing plays

defensive lineman: a player at the front of the defense

division: a group of teams in the NFL who play one another twice each season

draft: when teams take turns choosing new players

fumble: when a player loses hold of the ball while handling or running with it

interception: a pass caught by the opposing team that results in a change of possession

offensive lineman: a player positioned at the front of the offense whose job is to block defensive players

Pro Bowl: the NFL's all-star game

Pro Football Hall of Fame: a museum in Canton, Ohio, that honors the best players in football history

sack: when the quarterback is tackled for a loss of yards

safety: a defender who usually plays at the back of the defense

LEARN MORE

Ellenport, Craig. *The Story of the Minnesota Vikings*. Minnetonka, MN: Kaleidoscope, 2020.

Minnesota Vikings
https://www.vikings.com

Minnesota Vikings in the Pro Football Hall of Fame
https://www.profootballhof.com/teams/minnesota-vikings/

Ryan, Todd. *Minnesota Vikings*. Minneapolis: SportsZone, 2019.

Scheff, Matt. *The Super Bowl: Football's Game of the Year*. Minneapolis: Lerner Publications, 2021.

Sports Illustrated Kids—Football
https://www.sikids.com/football

INDEX

Carter, Cris, 21, 23, 29

Eller, Carl, 20

Favre, Brett, 17

Gjallarhorn, 9, 25

Grant, Bud, 12, 21

Metropolitan Stadium, 10

Moss, Randy, 23, 29

Page, Alan, 20

Peterson, Adrian, 16, 23, 29

Purple People Eaters, 5, 15, 20

Randle, John, 23, 29

Super Bowl, 5–6, 15–17, 19, 21, 26

Tarkenton, Fran, 11–12, 19

U.S. Bank Stadium, 25

PHOTO ACKNOWLEDGMENTS

Image credits: Bettmann/Contributor/Getty Images, p.4; Diamond Images/Contributor/Getty Images, p.6; Focus On Sport / Contributor/Getty Images, p.7; Star Tribune via Getty Images/Contributor/Getty Images, p.8; Underwood Archives/Contributor/Getty Images, p.9; Focus On Sport/Contributor/Getty Images, p.10; Clifton Boutelle/Contributor/Getty Images, p.11; Focus On Sport/Contributor/Getty Images, p.12; Michael Zagaris/Contributor/Getty Images, p.13; Martin Mills/Contributor/Getty Images, p.14; Focus On Sport/Contributor/Getty Images, p.15; Vincent Laforet/Staff/Getty Images, p.16; Icon Sportswire/Contributor/Getty Images, p.17; PAUL BUCK/Contributor/Getty Images, p.18; Focus On Sport/Contributor/Getty Images, p.19; Focus On Sport/Contributor/Getty Images, p.20; Focus On Sport/Contributor/Getty Images, p.21; Star Tribune via Getty Images/Contributor/Getty Images, p.22; Wesley Hitt/Stringer//Getty Images, p.23; David Berding/Stringer/Getty Images, p.24; Star Tribune via Getty Images/Contributor/Getty Images, p.25; David Berding/Contributor/Getty Images, p.26; Kevin Sabitus/Contributor/Getty Images, p.27; Joel Auerbach/Contributor/Getty Images, p.28;

Design element: Master3D/Shutterstock.com.

Cover image: Icon Sportswire/ContributorGetty Images